Chakras

This Is A Detailed Manual On The Seven Chakras, Specifically Designed For Individuals Who Are New To The Subject

(Engage In Chakra Meditation, Chakra Balancing, Aura Strengthening, And Energy Radiation With The Ultimate Crash Course)

Rainer Kloiber

TABLE OF CONTENT

Radiating Love Meditation 1

Five Myths Regarding The Third Eye And The Reasons Why The Media Is Trying To Keep You Sleeping. 13

Self-Awareness And Introspection: 41

Is The Chakra Of Your Third Eye In Alignment? 85

Mantra Progression And The Guru-Disciple Bond 153

Radiating Love Meditation

Do we truly love anyone else or ourselves? Answering this question is typically far more difficult than it seems at first. The majority of us can agree that enjoying who we are—our bodies, our lives, our thoughts, all of us—can positively impact our health, ourselves, and every other being we interact with daily. This practice allows you to build the part of you that can love unconditionally right now, no matter where you are, in opening your heart to yourself and others.

Spiral chambers that we will touch on in this exercise: In particular, chamber 14 (Loving Kindness)

◆◆◆

Nyasa and Meditation in Silence

In this meditation, we employ the energetic balancing and inward-looking of the senses techniques from yoga nidra. This meditation provides a professionally guided method in and out of the meditation state and a silent platform for 15 minutes for your self-directed meditation technique, mantra recitation, or visualization practice (yoga, sports, manifestation).

Through this practice, we touch on the following Spiral Chambers: Any chambers you desire, depending on the method you decide on for the silent portion.

◆◆◆ Meditation on Breath Freedom

One of the hardest things to do in breath meditation is to let our breath come naturally while we observe it. The major focus of this exercise is silently observing the breath while gradually letting go of the need to regulate it. It's a traditional mindfulness practice.

Spiral chambers that are discussed in this exercise: From 7 (Awareness) to 10 (Non-Judgement), every chamber

Course on Chakras

Through nine chakra-specific yoga nidra activities, this nine-week course examines our tantric chakra system. It helps you experience and balance your innermost energies freshly and profoundly.

All of the Spiral's chambers are covered in this course.

The Most Common Errors People Make When Seeking to Open the Third Eye

It is erroneous if there is anything worse than doing nothing at all. Activating the third eye works in the same way. You will have negative sensations if you attempt to awaken your third eye improperly. A powerful exercise, third eye awakening demands meticulous attention to detail and much perseverance.

You will be in the wrong place if you're hoping for quick fixes or instant satisfaction. Some people never seem to be able to fully activate their third eye, despite their constant attempts. It's not that they lack the third sight; rather, they seem to be searching in the wrong place. Inadequate comprehension or misreading of the indicators may result in despair or failure.

Some blunders people made upon opening their third eye are listed below. You should try to stay away from them.

Consuming False Information

Internet, TV, and other media are excellent resources for disseminating false information. They have a talent for exaggerating small issues. They have the power to convince you of ridiculous ideas that could ultimately drive you to despair. You must prepare for what lies ahead when you activate your third sight. Don't set unrealistic or low expectations. One can always avoid slipping into a gap by judging it. Before you start the process of opening your third eye, make sure you finish your homework.

Insufficient Trust

Trust is a vital component of any travel, but it becomes even more important when it involves adventure. Activating your third eye is like embarking on a journey you have never experienced. You must believe in yourself and your intuition to feel it. When you activate your third eye, it would be beneficial to not doubt anything you feel or see. It would also be beneficial to appropriately value the changes you encounter along the journey. It's critical to stay aware of even the tiniest of happenings.

Absence of Intent

Individuals who don't have a clear reason for opening their third eye will not succeed. Reaching the third eye is not an easy feat. It's not something you can brush off like you can other things. Certain irreversible processes are initiated. Knowing exactly why you were opening your third eye would be beneficial. You won't be able to assess your success in your endeavors until then. You might not find anything if you are not searching for something specific.

Insufficient Methodology

It is crucial to use the right approach to activate the third eye. Activating the third eye may appear to follow an unclear path. There is no set path for the voyage within, yet it is crucial to use the right technique, or you risk becoming lost. Please select the best approach for you and adhere to it closely. If you constantly alter your plans, you cannot succeed. Continue practicing regularly and with great devotion. Individuals who treat this casually wind up squandering their time.

Too Much Effort

Try not to exert too much effort. People who are eager to succeed quickly frequently make excessive initial attempts. It could cause desperation and cause your mind to fabricate stories that ultimately lead to failure. Concentrate on the method when using the third eye and allow things to unfold independently. Never try to make your mind imagine something or think a certain way. You may form incorrect beliefs about imagery if you rely too much on imagery. You could begin to see the things you desire to see without making any progress.

Give up Seeking the Incorrect Indications

If you looked for the right indicators, it would be helpful. Certain purported experts have associated incorrect ideas with the third eye activation technique. They have led people to assume certain indicators are necessary for third-eye activation. This is not true. Pay attention to the minute alterations occurring within you. Take the initiative and follow your gut. Do not rely on false assumptions. Your third eye awakening experience may be unique from others. You might never be content if you never stop searching for the affairs.

No Quick Fix

Activating the third eye is not like placing an online order. It takes time for it to occur. It could take a while to see a noticeable shift, even after your third eye has awakened. It takes considerably longer and a lot of practice to hone your skills. This is something that you need to focus on closely.

Insufficient Experience

This builds on the last point that was made. You must practice your talents for a considerable time to see quantifiable outcomes. If you don't consistently practice using your third eye, it won't have a big impact, even if it is active. Your mind needs to be trained to focus in the appropriate direction. Your brain needs to train itself to identify the cues. It must be able to view things more perceptively. You can only achieve all of this by practicing consistently. Include meditation in your daily routine. Don't let yourself down or make up an excuse. You will only be bringing failure to your goal if you do this.

Don't Overpublicize Your Work

A personal mission is needed to open your third eye. The voyage is lengthy, and there are always bumps in the road. You have to refrain from discussing it with your pals. These conversations elicit envy and condemnation. Doubts may arise due to being called names or made fun of. Kindly keep it private and continue honing your skills. It is among the greatest strategies for maintaining good vibes and achieving greater outcomes.

Five Myths Regarding The Third Eye And The Reasons Why The Media Is Trying To Keep You Sleeping.

People frequently have incorrect ideas about concepts they don't fully comprehend. In the past, those aware of the third eye's abilities advanced quickly in society. The third eye endowed them with even greater intelligence, insight, and prescience. Being able to see more clearly than others is a gift that has numerous uses. Those in authority frequently desire to maintain their position and require subjugation.

These factors contribute to society's extreme ignorance about the third eye notion. It is evident from evidence and symbolism that the concept of the third eye was known to all civilizations.

The pineal gland resembles a pinecone in shape. Scientific understanding of the pineal gland's significance in human anatomy was unavailable to ancient societies. They knew this gland could have some incredible feats, though. All cultures' portrayals of the pinecone as the third eye have no alternative explanation.

During the mummification process, the ancient Egyptians maintained the pineal gland independently. They wouldn't have gone to such an effort without recognizing its importance. The third eye is depicted in their artwork and artifacts. Although Egyptian culture accomplished some amazing things in their day, it was believed that they relied too much on magical abilities.

Pinecones are also depicted as being carried by Greek gods. Historical artwork and artifacts make extensive use of this symbolism.

Likewise with the Babylonians. Babylonian gods hold pinecones.

Eastern cultures have provided evidence that they were aware of the third eye's mysteries. Traditions from both Buddhism and Hinduism demonstrate that they were aware of the third eye. Shiva, one of the most well-known Hindu figures, is shown as having a third physical eye. With this eye, he is supposed to be able to see into the past, present, and future. Adherents of this faith also think that Lord Shiva has the power to open his eyes and either create or destroy the world.

In Buddhist tradition, the third eye is revered greatly. It holds that the origin of higher consciousness is the third eye. Breaking out from the cycle of birth and death has always been highly valued in our society. It holds that achieving "Nirvana," or escape from the cycle of life, is the main purpose of existence. According to Buddhist tradition, achieving Nirvana is contingent upon having no "Karma" that binds one to the world. They think that they can reach this condition with the aid of greater consciousness.

An Instructional Guided Throat Chakra Meditation

After settling into a comfortable posture, gently close your eyes. Breathe deeply in, then ease into your posture as you release the breath and let go of any stored tension in your body. Visualize your energy easily flowing through the chakras, and imagine your base chakra grounded.

Turn your focus to your throat. Imagine a bright, glistening blue light emanating from this area, radiating honesty and clarity. Observe as this light expands to include your entire neck region, bringing balance and healing energy.

Return your focus to your breathing when you take a breath and release it. As you take in the soft breeze, let your nose pick up on all the aromas surrounding you. As you take a deeper breath, let your body experience peace and relaxation.

Let's now examine the topic of telling the truth. Consider the influence and significance of genuine and honest communication. Consider instances when you might have been suppressing the truth or failing to stand up for your convictions. Treat yourself well, and don't criticize yourself during these times.

Imagine the blue light in your throat chakra growing brighter and more vibrant as you take deep breaths. Feel this light rising through your whole being, enabling you to speak your truth and find your voice.

Imagine any anxieties or insecurities that have kept you from expressing yourself freely being dispelled by this dazzling blue light. You can speak honestly and clearly as your self-assurance and sense of empowerment grow.

Turn your attention to the idea of self-expression now. Think about the special abilities, concepts, and gifts you have. Accept that the world needs to hear your voice and that you have something important to say.

Take a moment to decide that you will express yourself freely and authentically. Imagine the blue light growing within your throat chakra, making room for your expression of self in a loving and spacious manner. As you let your genuine self come through in your words and deeds, experience a sense of independence and liberty.

Accept that the world is a better place because of your genuineness. You give others the confidence and inspiration to be authentic by being yourself. Give up trying to make excuses for who you are.

Let's now work on developing an open mind. Consider how important it is to hear other people's viewpoints and to keep an open mind to fresh concepts.

Recognize any inclination you may have to think rigidly or exclusively. Don't focus on them; let these ideas go as you breathe.

Spend time deciding that you want to develop an open mind. Imagine the blue light in your throat chakra becoming larger and larger until it forms an area of openness and curiosity. Have an open mind and be prepared to examine fresh perspectives and concepts.

Accept that being receptive to new ideas and willing to learn from others are the keys to genuine development and understanding. Let go of preconceived assumptions or prejudices so fresh perspectives and knowledge might enter your life.

Let's now investigate the idea of active listening. Is it true that you pay attention to what others say when they speak? Consider the importance of genuinely listening to and comprehending what people are saying. While listening, note any inclinations you may have to interrupt or pass judgment.

Decide to take up the habit of actively listening as you keep breathing. Imagine the blue light in your neck chakra rising even higher, forming a realm of profound awareness and presence. Empathize and care for others while listening to them with an open mind and heart.

Accept that by actively listening to people, you enable them to express themselves in a secure and encouraging way. You may promote harmony, understanding, and connection in your relationships by actively listening to each other.

Feel the blue light in your throat chakra becoming more intense than before while you concentrate on breathing deeply. Feel its truth and clarity resonate through your body. Accept that you bring harmony into your life and relationships with others when you speak your truth, express yourself honestly, practice open-mindedness, and practice active listening.

Take a minute to appreciate your generated blue energy and let it align your throat chakra. This will facilitate honest and transparent speech, self-expression, receptiveness, and attentive listening.

Recognize that you can listen with compassion and understanding and express yourself honestly. Embrace the beauty of genuine and emotional communication and have faith in the intelligence of your voice.

When ready, return your focus to your physical body with gentleness. Gently open your eyes and wiggle your toes and fingers. Give your communication, self-expression, open-mindedness, and active listening some thought and nurture them. Utilize your fresh energy to fulfill your communication aims while keeping your intentions in mind.

(Third Day)

Inhale deeply and slowly for a long moment. As you release the breath, shift your focus to the base of your spine. Imagine a red chakra blazing brightly right now. Your mind and heart are calmed by the warmth and shine of this chakra, enabling you to completely experience the security and tranquility it offers.

Feel steady and rooted, as if the earth is holding a large, warm rock. Imagine standing peacefully at the foot of a snow-capped mountain, watching it gently rise toward the sky. A huge opening in front of you leads to a cave. As you approach the cave, the sun's rays appear appealing.

Move ahead and enter the cave by taking one step. It will be evident that the cave has a very high ceiling and smooth walls. The breeze is warm, soothing, and gentle, making you feel at ease. Take a few more steps and pay attention to your surroundings.

Now, you see a walkway leading to a large, circular room. A big, rectangular rock is positioned in the center.

Proceed to the rock and settle down on it. You'll be able to sit cross-legged naturally.

At this point, you feel like a part of the mountain, like an appendage. You experience a strong sense of anchoring yourself to the soil. You're secure. The soil supports and nurtures every part of who you are.

Your first chakra is spinning and getting more powerful, as you can see. A red light covers you, seeping into every cell and pore in your body as this chakra spins considerably more quickly.

Inhale deeply and let the energy sent toward the base of your spine feel.

In this mindful condition, let yourself go.

Now, gently stand up and exit the room by taking the passage that leads to the cave's exterior. Look back at the mountain and experience a sense of unity and connection.

You can rise and open your eyes when you're ready.

SACRAL CHAKRA

(The fourth day)

Assume a comfortable stance for yourself. Let your body as a whole unwind and find comfort if you're lying on the ground. Place your hands at your sides or thighs if seated in a chair.

Shut your eyes now. You have this time all to yourself. Let go of all your concerns. Give them up.

Recognize every sound around you and simply accept it as it is, without comment or judgment.

Feel the cool, gentle air gently brushing against the surface of your body. Notice the light and shadow seeping between your eyes.

Feel the earth beneath your feet, sustaining your body and weight and the vast expanses of sky above and below you.

Inhale deeply to purify yourself, and then exhale to release all the tension in your body and mind.

Just softly return your focus to your breathing whenever your thoughts divert you. Take conscious breaths in and out.

Now, focus on your lower abdomen. Imagine a lovely orange light moving in a manner reminiscent of a tiny pool. Pay attention to how this feels. How does it appear? What is this light's purpose? Does something feel tingly? Take note of your thoughts with gentleness. What is their speed? Do they cause you any trouble? Is orange something you can picture in your mind?

Now, return your focus to your breathing. Inhale serenity and exhale stress and resistance. Breathe the warm orange light of now into yourself. Observe how this light enters your sacral chakra right at the center of your abdomen. Permit this energy to permeate your environment. Warm regards and good vibes.

Please accept all of the joyous emotions that this orange light gives.

Inhale happiness and exhale all of your internal tension. (Repeat rhythmically.)

It's time to block off this chakra now. Focus solely on your lower belly and the orange light associated with the sacral chakra. Observe how this light is decreasing until it reaches the tiny size of a fairy's light. Return this light to its regular operation. Say the mantra aloud: "My sacral chakra is now functioning normally."

Bring your attention to the calm, gentle rhythm of your breathing. Inhale and exhale in a rhythmic pattern. Feel the cool air completely fill your lungs as it goes down your throat and nose.

Observe how your tummy moves naturally and softly when you breathe in and out. Feel at ease knowing that the floor or your chair supports your complete body. Focus just on your hands and move them at a slow pace. Experience this movement on a physical level.

If your shoulders are stiff, shrug them off and let them drop gradually. Take note of the room's temperature and listen to all surrounding noises.

When you're ready, slowly stand up and open your eyes.

William

William, a 40-year-old guy, has been battling a sacral chakra block. It had never been easy for William to be happy, convey his feelings, and keep up good relationships. He frequently felt his creativity was restricted and that he had no passion or enjoyment in life.

William's sacral chakra blockage resulted from the emotional suppression he experienced as a child and a lack of encouragement for his artistic expression. He was raised to believe that his sentiments were unimportant or invalid, which caused him to repress them and lose touch with his creative spirit.

William began a healing path to balance his sacral chakra after realizing how his blocked chakra affected his general health.

1. Emotional Recovery:

William's emotional wounds needed to be addressed and healed before he could begin to mend his blocked sacral chakra. To examine and process his repressed feelings from the past, he sought the assistance of a therapist who specialized in emotional recovery. William overcame emotional obstacles and learned more about the causes of his emotional patterns through therapy.

2. Artistic Expression:

William did various creative things to clear his sacral chakra and rekindle his creative flame. He dabbled in various artistic mediums, including writing, painting, and music-making. He could release his inhibitions and express himself freely through these activities, clearing the obstructions in his sacral chakra.

3. Sensuality and Enjoyment:

William realized that to heal his sacral chakra, he needed to be in touch with his senses and enjoy life. He experimented with techniques, including sensuous hobbies, dancing, and mindful eating that made him happy. He reactivated his pleasure center and strengthened his sense of self through deliberate savoring of sensory sensations.

4. Techniques for Releasing Emotions:

William used various emotional release techniques to clear his sacral chakra of pent-up emotions and energy. He used breathwork techniques, taking deep breaths and exhalations to let go of any emotions holding onto space in his energy core. He also experimented with methods like physical therapy and EFT (Emotional Freedom Technique) to integrate and release more repressed emotions.

5. Therapeutic Approaches:

William sought the help of bodyworkers and energy healers to help him restore his sacral chakra. His sacral chakra was cleared and balanced through regular Reiki sessions, improving his emotional and creative energy flow. Additionally, acupuncture and massage therapy assisted in easing his tension and enhancing the flow of energy throughout his body.

6. Building Good Relationships:

William understood that it was critical to build genuine, healthy relationships to facilitate the healing of his sacral chakra. He concentrated on fostering connections with people who supported his creative activities and encouraged him to communicate his emotions. Through establishing a supportive network, he established a secure environment that fostered the growth of his creative energy and emotions.

As William committed to his recovery process over time, his sacral chakra opened and flowed more freely. His existence took on a profoundly different meaning. He became more adept at expressing his feelings and rediscovered his love of artistic endeavors. He created more satisfying and close relationships and felt more joy and pleasure daily.

William was able to clear his blocked sacral chakra by going after the underlying reasons for it and using a holistic therapy method. He keeps the equilibrium and vitality he has developed by making his mental health, artistic expression, and caring relationships his top priorities. William's path exemplifies how emotional healing, creative expression, self-awareness, and energetic alignment may bring the sacral chakra back into balance and improve general well-being.

Emily

A 32-year-old lady, Emily has been battling a blocked chakra in her solar plexus. Emily struggled to establish herself in many aspects of her life and suffered from low self-esteem and lack of confidence. She struggled to create boundaries and frequently felt unsure of herself.

Emily's solar plexus chakra blockage resulted from the criticism and invalidation she experienced as a child. She was taught as a child that other people's thoughts and opinions didn't matter, which made her repress her authority and grow afraid of rejection.

After seeing how her blocked solar plexus chakra affected her health, Emily set out on a therapeutic path to clear this energy center.

Self-Awareness And Introspection:

To clear Emily's blocked solar plexus chakra, self-reflection and awareness-building were the first things to do. It took her some time to pinpoint the ideas and cognitive processes undermining her sense of self-efficacy. She developed a deeper comprehension of the underlying reasons for her impediment and how it materialized in her life through journaling and self-inquiry.

2. Developing Self-Belief:

Emily adopted self-love and self-acceptance routines as a means of boosting her confidence. She repeated empowering phrases that regularly validated her value and ability as part of her positive affirmation practice. She also surrounded herself with people who acknowledged and praised her strengths, people who were encouraging and supportive.

3. Establishing Limits:

Emily realized that to heal her solar plexus chakra, establishing healthy limits was critical. She practiced recognizing her needs and expressing them to other people in an assertive manner. She prioritized self-care and practiced saying no when it was called for. Her solar plexus chakra unlocked as she reclaimed her sense of control and self-respect through setting limits.

4. Empowerment Techniques:

Emily did things that strengthened her to bolster her power. She went to seminars and workshops centered on empowerment and personal growth. She also got involved in things outside her comfort zone, such as leadership positions and public speaking. She was able to regain her power and confidence thanks to these exercises.

5. Exercises for Core Strength:

Emily's physical regimen included core strength exercises to aid in healing her solar plexus chakra. She did yoga poses, including warrior III and boat pose, to strengthen the stomach region. She also did Pilates and planks, two workouts emphasizing strengthening the core. Her solar plexus chakra was brought into balance as she strengthened her physical core, which reflected the strengthening of her energy core.

6. Therapeutic Approaches:

Emily looked to energy healers and chakra-healing therapists for assistance. She underwent Reiki sessions and energy cleansing to eliminate any energetic obstructions in her solar plexus chakra. She also looked into therapeutic approaches like cognitive-behavioral therapy to address limiting ideas and replace them with empowering thoughts.

As Emily committed to her healing process, her solar plexus chakra opened and flowed more freely over time. Her life took a drastic turn for the better. She became more forceful and confident, feeling more in control of her destiny. Her relationships improved in harmony and deference as a result of her decision-making, which was clear and strong.

Through empowering techniques and addressing the root causes of her obstruction, Emily was able to repair her blocked solar plexus chakra. She keeps incorporating these routines into her everyday life to preserve the equilibrium and self-determination she has developed. Emily's story serves as an example of the ability of introspection, empowerment, and energetic healing to bring harmony back to

Make use of healing crystals.

Subtle and physical assistants can ease the shift into awareness while you're clearing subtle and physical energy obstructions and flows. Consider crystals as an example. All these earth minerals, whether polished or raw, are alive and vibrating. These vibrations can directly impart healing properties to you when you hold them about you (particularly if you are very weak in those vibrations). If you hold a healing crystal in your hands, you might experience an increased capacity for tolerance, love, dedication, trust, or other qualities. This crystal healing has enormous potential for kundalini awakening as well. Chakras are associated with various colors of crystals, and certain crystals possess the extraordinary capacity to simultaneously align and purify all seven chakras. I suggest using crystal healing if you feel like your process needs a boost. It's simple, enjoyable, and has nearly immediate results.

Engage in random acts of kindness or give back.

One way to align your frequency with what Kundalini can work with is to give as selflessly as possible. Engage in sporadic acts of generosity and give back whenever you can. Check what has and has not been returned. Examine what resurfaces even after it has been sent out. Kundalini (and the Shakti that gives it life) will take notice if you operate with this compassionate spirit and send energy out into the world like a boomerang waiting to come back somehow. These routines might eventually come naturally to you, or they might even bring tangible benefits closer to the time of your first action. Send as much selflessness and generosity as possible into the universe, and then watch to see what comes back. If all you get back is understanding and information, be grateful! Nothing at all had to be the case. As you strive to live without attachments and unreasonable expectations, putting these techniques into practice could be challenging, but only if it presents a lesson you need to learn.

First, meditate to clear, align, and open your chakras.

Even if it seems easy, you can always begin your day by opening, clearing, and aligning all of your chakras as best you can with yourself. This technique can help you immensely, especially if you're comfortable cleansing your chakras and have a lot of meditation experience. Try to begin your day every day with a chakra cleaning and a shower. Imagine that obstructions flow out of each chakra, down to your feet, and into the water that drains as the water touches you. Every time you take a shower, picture yourself feeling more attuned to your chakras and envision yourself feeling entire and at peace within after this cleanse is finished. Starting the day this way can greatly improve your wakeup and give Kundalini a better move for the remainder of your waking hours.

Engage in active forgiveness and patience.

Often, our strongest resentment is what prevents us from waking up. Having a grudge is usually spiritually harmful, even though it can remind some people of their power and ability to shape their world. They are typically associated with heart chakra blockages, which can be resolved by making bold and active declarations of love, tolerance, and forgiveness. Try to be a better person the next time you butt into your grudges or the people who are connected to them. But don't simply think that way; live your life as a "better person" without feeling or thinking that you are "better" than you are. Give up resentment. Reject fear, frustration, annoyance, rage, and envy. Try your best to show love, forgiveness, and acceptance despite their harshness. You'll grow spiritually and emotionally if you can roll with the punches.

With your lover, engage in tantric sex.

Although having sex is not the only way to awaken your Kundalini, some sexual activities can help you feel more shakti and raise your Kundalini. One of the healthiest and most fruitful sexual practices associated with kundalini awakening is tantric sex, in particular. The objective of climax will be slightly different during tantric sex, but you and your lover will attempt various positions together and mostly engage in the same activities as usual. To put it in very Western terms, tantric sex is about retaining sexual postures, holding or diverting orgasm, and stretching endurance to its extremes. By taking and maintaining these positions, you will create energy between the two of you and direct that energy upward into your chakras rather than outward, as it were. Actions of this kind immediately involve your Kundalini. Hence, this ancient sexual technique may be closely linked to the awakening of your Kundalini.

Try experiencing orgasm differently.

Try focusing your orgasm on a different portion of your body to trigger awakening if you frequently have orgasms but don't yet comprehend tantric sex or want to practice it. You will attempt to direct your orgasmic energy upwards, through your chakras one after the other, to your crown, as opposed to outward and down through your base, just as the pair doing tantric sex and experiencing an orgasm. When you push this creative energy out of your body through the root chakra after an orgasm, it always leaves your body. However, if you reroute some of that energy upwards, you can invite the snake to move and save some for yourself.

Six Other Helpful Practices

You can benefit from adding six or seven extra intense practices to your daily program in addition to the 29 kundalini boosters. Here are some pathways to apply to your awakening to enhance, deepen, and heighten the experience, ranging from physical activity to dietary changes and other forms of subtle energy healing. Everything depends on what you are willing to attract into your life and what makes you feel at ease.

Get moving and run.

You could begin running if your physical condition permits. Running has several advantages for the body outside the cardiovascular and musculoskeletal systems. Running can help you connect spiritually with your ability to change the world and temporarily break free. You may feel you could run forever when you're in the zone and your stride flows naturally. This makes me very happy and helps me overcome other feelings of imprisonment by the system. Some people find that running helps them get the release they need while improving their physical capabilities. Running regularly can enhance your general health and well-being, strength, endurance, and posture. Should you be experiencing difficulties with any of these three areas, even after you have recently begun running, you may want to give it another go. The goal of enhancing your general health is undermined if you're burdening yourself with needless stress. It is advised for these individuals to look for other outdoor physical activities besides running, like biking, rollerblading, road walking, trail walking, and so forth.

Why Is the Root Chakra Blocked?

Various factors might block your root chakra, but spiritual, physical, and emotional. Since the root chakra is linked to every other chakra, whatever issues you may be experiencing with it will probably also impact the other chakras.

Emotional obstacles can take many forms, such as harboring grudges against people or simply not feeling like you belong. Unhealthy lifestyle choices such as smoking or consuming excessive amounts of alcohol can result in physical obstructions; your body becomes clogged, and your energy centers begin to shut down one by one. A person may experience spiritual obstacles for various reasons, such as not realizing they are on a spiritual path or not feeling prepared to connect with God or the cosmos. To solve this, you don't have to convert to a religion. All you have to do is accept that there is something greater than yourself in the cosmos and have faith in the divine or the universe. Whatever you choose to name this power, admitting its existence is a positive first step.

When your Root Chakra is balanced and awake, how does it feel?

When your root chakra is in balance, you can feel grounded in the now and connected to your body and the world around you. You can sense life's energy within you, making you more self-assured, inventive, impulsive, and strong. You can deeply express yourself in a way that allows others to get to know you better, leading to warm and loving connections with others.

Life can provide excitement, which can help you believe in your goals and discover a method to achieve them. You can make judgments with greater strength and confidence because you are not afraid of the consequences for you or those around you. This is a crucial aspect of your energy as things get exciting. In addition, you'll start to feel more confident about your life and enjoy success and plenty in all you accomplish.

Affirmations & Mantras to Clear the Root Chakra

Using mantras and affirmations is always beneficial when trying to clear your root chakra. It can assist you in narrowing down your intention, increasing your chances of removing the energy obstruction preventing you from progressing.

These affirmations are available for use:

"Knowing everything is well gives me peace of mind."

"I am not a victim anymore."

"I have faith in my ability to move in the direction of my dreams."

"I respect whatever actions I must take to achieve my goals. I respect both my soul and my higher self.

"I let go of everything that prevents me from leading a happy and meaningful life."

"I base every choice I make on my deepest desires and thoughts. I'm free. I have self-confidence.

"I have faith in my ability to act morally. I rely on my gut feeling to lead me.

When people try to pull me back, I find the strength to keep going. I decide to forgive myself and move on from my previous transgressions. I'm starting over.

"I don't feel trapped anymore, but I'm also not going too fast. I am simply and firmly moving towards my goals on a steady route.

"I make all of my decisions because they are consistent with the identity I have established for myself. I have a solid sense of who I am. My life is in harmony, and my mind is clear.

LAM is the most effective mantra to utilize when working with this chakra. This can be chanted aloud or silently in your thoughts. To be clear, this is pronounced L-Ah-M rather than "lamb." You can sing it in the key of C to increase its impact. You can also chant "Oh."

Oils and Crystals

Consider working with garnet, hematite, ruby, carnelian, and black obsidian. You can use the rocks in your hands for meditation or just wear them as jewelry. You can also do meditation using the color red. You can use essential oils like pineapple, jasmine, geranium, patchouli, camphor, sandalwood, and rose.

The Root Chakra via Breathwork

These are the ideal types of pranayama for the Muladhara:

Sitali pranayama, commonly known as the cooling breath

Alternatively known as Nadishodhana, alternate nostril breathing

Calm Breath

Choose a comfortable position to sit in. Your spine is long and graceful, your shoulders should be relaxed, and your stomach should remain soft. Shut your eyes gently.

Breathe in through your nose and out again. Repeat this three times as you give your body and mind time to relax into the present.

Press your lips together.

If you can manage it, shape your tongue into a taco and stick it out of your mouth. If this isn't possible, you can still make a small circle with your lips pursed and open. To create a channel that makes it easy for your breath to pass through, keep your tongue pressed against your lower teeth. As an alternative, you might press it up to your upper teeth.

Take your time and slowly inhale through pursed lips. Give your tummy and chest enough room to fill with air (this is why your stomach muscles need to remain soft).

Once the air has filled your lungs and abdomen, slowly exhale via your nose while keeping your mouth shut.

To maximize the benefits of this breathwork, perform five to ten more repetitions. Each session should consist of 26 repetitions in the morning and evening. If you aren't comfortable performing so many reps, you can work up to that amount.

Your Form

This was the aspect that took me the longest to figure out when I was trying to get over my panic attacks. I drank a bottle of Coke every day when I was older. I had one right next to my bed. I felt that water was for fish. I consumed a bag of Doritos and anything else I desired daily. The TV commercials I watched suggested everyone else was doing it, so why should I be any different?

My doctor never once inquired about what I ate or drank when I discussed my panic episodes with him. Then Amadeus, my dog, fell ill one day. He wasn't feeling well and had a bloated head. I immediately brought him to the vet.

Before even checking Amadeus out, the veterinarian asked me what I had been feeding him as I placed him on the table for additional examination. Perplexed, I responded to the query. As it turned out, I was overfeeding Amadeus leftovers and snacks that weren't meant for dogs. Even though his weight was normal, it was causing inflammation and other health issues.

"I'm sure what I eat will have significant effects on me, too, if nutrition can have bad effects on my dog." Thus, why didn't my physician inquire about my dietary habits?"Believe me and the hundreds of individuals I have assisted—your body and emotions are greatly influenced by the food and beverages you consume!

Indeed. What you eat and drink may have a role in contributing to your anxiety and panic episodes. Furthermore, calories and weight are not the topic of discussion here.

Coffee

Caffeine acts in your body similarly to adrenaline, increasing stress levels, causing your nervous system to become more sensitive, and disrupting your circadian rhythm. It is also among the main reasons why adrenal exhaustion occurs.

You'll stay focused, aware, and sharp with caffeine. For some people who would otherwise be sleepwalking, that is fantastic. However, those who are more prone to anxiety, like you and me, will become so sensitive and tense that little will be needed to cause real discomfort or perhaps a panic attack. Caffeine in little doses won't likely trigger panic attacks on its own, but it will make them much easier to occur!

For this reason, chocolate in general—even pure, 100% cacao—should be prohibited. It has levels of theobromine, a chemical that can quicken your heartbeat and give you jitters, and caffeine.

Reduce your daily caffeine intake to zero tea or any other caffeinated beverage. Avoid quitting abruptly, as this may cause severe headaches that last for a few days.

And if you're thinking, "Nope, that's not it! I've been drinking it for a very long time. Please try it and tell me I'm incorrect. Reintroduce it after four weeks of abstinence; you'll immediately notice the negative effects of caffeine.

The Avoidance and Elastic Comfort Circle

The comfort zone can be expanded but will contract back down when you stop stretching its bounds, much like an elastic band.

Everything seems completely normal within your comfort zone, and you don't have to cope with any worries or anxiety. I hope basic tasks like boiling water and cleaning your teeth are within your purview. It's probably not a good idea to clip wild alligators' toenails.

Anything beyond the circle necessitates more diligent work. To you, it's unfamiliar, unclear, or perhaps plain frightening. When you were initially learning to drive, learning to cross a busy intersection was not something you were comfortable with. And so driving in various traffic patterns falls well within the circle if your worry is not driving itself.

You will need to work hard. This is challenging since your fear and resistance will increase as you approach the edge. Your body is attempting to alert you to the possible threat. The goal, then, is to experience the anxiety without letting it overcome you. Continue to persevere.

The majority of life's enjoyment is found beyond that dread.

For this reason, anxiety and panic episodes are brought on by avoidance. Avoidance is only a temporary fix. What better approach to prevent another panic attack if performing X caused you anxiety or a panic attack than to never perform X again?

From what we've seen, this is not the answer. Because it is elastic, your comfort zone will gradually get smaller. You'll find that more and more situations or things frighten you, so you'll have to avoid them as well. Before you realize it, simple tasks like changing the toilet paper roll could become stressful. One of the biggest blunders I made was this downhill spiral. That explains why my initial mild anxiety eventually developed into complete agoraphobia, causing me to spend as much time as possible at home. The stretchy comfort circle drew closer to me as I avoided what worried me.

By avoiding what frightens you, you give it power. It shouldn't have had power! You're admitting that it's harmful and that your anxiety is valid if you're avoiding it. That is the exact opposite of the answer.

I know that avoiding something can be beneficial. It can instantly relieve anxiety and stop panic attacks, which is a miraculous result.

Since trying to control everything is a kind of avoidance, it also belongs in this chapter. "I have to make sure I sit in the aisle," "Okay, I'll go, but I have to make sure there are restrooms nearby," "Let me Google street view the entire location before I say yes so I can prepare," or "Okay as long as someone is with me or is standing by so I can call them." You can deceive yourself into thinking everything will be okay because you can painstakingly anticipate and plan every scenario that could occur. But what happens if something is still missed?

The good news is that it will never get dull if you approach life intending to control everything. This will exacerbate your anxiousness and further tax your delicate nervous system. Rarely will things go as planned.

However, I want to make a more profound point: you don't need to be in charge of everything. The source of the anxiety and possibly the panic attack is not the place, the circumstance, or even the individuals. You and I are in this together. We use our minds for it.

Having everything under control only makes it harder for you to suppress your worry; it doesn't help you. However, it remains present and will become extremely acute should things not go according to plan, which is bound to happen.

In the book's second half, we shall address a superior method. For the time being, please be aware that two common causes of generalized anxiety are the idea that you should control everything and that you should only leave your comfort zone.

Shame is the root cause.

The server placed my plate in front of me while sitting in a restaurant with several colleagues. The aroma of the tagliatellefrutti di mare that I had ordered filled my senses with deliciousness. I tasted it and found it enjoyable. Then, a few seconds later, I started to feel sick to my stomach. My mouth began to wet, and my stomach rejected any more food. "Am I about to pass out? I questioned worriedly.

Let's rewind a bit. The panic that was ready to overwhelm me appears to have been brought on by the sickness.

Was it, though?

"Why is this occurring right now, Djeezs? I mean, my plate is still incredibly full. I'm eating nonstop right now! The waiter will question me about what went wrong if I do. I'm going to make the chef feel bad! Assuming that this wasn't a freezer meal that he had reheated, however, my colleagues... Watch them gobble away! Why don't I resemble them? They're loving this and having a good time. What if I have to puke right here and now? That will definitely be the end of my career. That's it; my dignity is gone! Alternatively, I may ask to be excused and dash to the toilet. Who does that in the middle of a dinner, though, so it's not ideal either? Moreover, my mother has always advised me not to sprint in restaurants! Come on, Geert—that isn't appropriate conduct, and thinking like that isn't appropriate either! Give a damn and act regular for once! I'm going to have to take action since it's becoming worse. How do I best conceal it?"

This would go on and on, and I would always grab a bite to eat when the nausea started to lessen. I would take a break and let them know I wasn't feeling well if it didn't go away. The issue was that I never felt great when we ate outside or in a group environment.

SHAME was the true cause; the nausea was only an unpleasant symptom, frequently brought on by certain ingredients my body was reacting to. I felt guilty about my feelings and not being like everyone else.

In this instance, my vicious anxiety cycle was sparked by shame; otherwise, I would have merely experienced nausea. If I had been eating by myself, I would have only felt sick instead of anxious.

You, too, I'm sure, are at least partially to blame for shame.

Those who have followed my coaching over the years, the majority of whom have never met me in person, tend to open up more quickly, which aids in their healing. These are a few embarrassing instances of folks I've met over the years:

- The woman who, anytime there was another person there, was terrified to handle a knife in the kitchen because she thought she would do something from horror films. Her anxiety was heightened by the concept alone. "I'm crazy; I must be crazy for having ideas like these," she would say. Naturally, the more she tried to suppress these ideas, the more they returned.

She wasn't insane. Everyone thinks absurd things. Simply said, other individuals are better at ignoring them and showing little concern. The issue was that she felt too embarrassed to discuss these ideas. If she had followed through on it, she would have discovered that others had also had them.

Still, she felt too embarrassed of herself to entertain such thoughts.

She wasn't alone; I've met plenty of women and men who share this anxiety and could teach "coming up with thrilling scenarios" to the likes of Stephen King.

- The mother who objected to being left alone with her child. She always desired the presence of her mother, husband, or anybody else. She lacked self-confidence. This mother thought that if she was left alone with her child, she would go insane or become incapable of providing for them.

- The pilot of the aircraft I mentioned earlier, who was frightened of flying. For obvious reasons, shame was a key factor in his situation.

Admitting to himself that, given his occupation, he felt afraid of this absurd thing was the first step towards healing. He confessed to me in this instance, but that was a vital and required first step towards his healing.

- A globally recognized football star who feared having a panic attack on the pitch, with millions of spectators observing his every move. Being a fierce football player, he was too embarrassed to acknowledge to anyone that he was afraid of this.

A father who had finally made good on his commitment to his wife and kids to take a vacation with them. His anxiousness skyrocketed weeks before the departure date because he was afraid he would have panic attacks and be unable to go home. He was so scared of spoiling their vacation that he ultimately did just that—canceling the entire trip ahead with the pathetic justification that he had too much work to do. He felt inadequate and heartbroken.

This is when you might start to notice a pattern. Most of these people thought no one else would understand their anxieties. They would not comprehend.

It seemed at first that there was some humiliation towards other people involved. However, the real reason is the far deeper guilt—the shame we have towards ourselves.

We truly feel ashamed of who we are when, for whatever reason, we cannot accept our shortcomings and errors. This profoundly affects our genuine core confidence and sense of self-worth.

The discrepancy between our true selves and the impression we wish people to have of us gives rise to anxiety.

Is The Chakra Of Your Third Eye In Alignment?

Have you ever experienced a time in your life when you were deeply pessimistic about the state of the world as a whole? Perhaps you had trouble believing in your strengths and capabilities. It's possible that you didn't feel connected to those around you. Or perhaps you were surrounded by supportive individuals but found it difficult to trust them. When the third eye chakra is out of harmony, it may be very unsettling since it offers us knowledge, understanding, and clarity about ourselves and the world around us.

You cannot advance in your spiritual journey if you are unaware of the possibilities linked to this chakra and the problems that arise from a blocked chakra. In this chapter, let's examine these details in more detail.

Signs of a Blocked Chakra in the Third Eye

To comprehend its symptoms, we must be conscious of a blocked third eye chakra's impact on our lives. Since this chakra is situated on the forehead and is intimately associated with hearing and vision, any obstruction in this chakra primarily affects these areas. Physical signs of a blocked third eye chakra include the following blurry or poor vision, or overall visual issues

problems with hearing

closed sinuses

Migraines and headaches

imbalance of hormones

Problems with metabolism

lightheadedness

Convulsions

problems with the nerves and spinal cord

As always, it's crucial to have a medical examination done to rule out any underlying medical issues. Never presume that a blockage in your third eye chakra is the cause of these problems.

There are also indications of a blocked third eye, such as mental and emotional disorders. Let's examine a few of these:

You may begin to experience memory problems. You may find it difficult to recall details precisely because memory and attention are closely related to our third eye. It could be challenging for you to concentrate on significant issues simultaneously.

You may be experiencing symptoms of a blocked third eye chakra if you are experiencing higher levels of anxiety than usual. Anxiety generally arises from feelings of uncertainty about our lives and ourselves. The fact is, we all have uncertain lives. We must have confidence in ourselves to go through its many highs and lows. When our third eye is closed, faith is replaced by uncertainty and bewilderment, which can exacerbate anxiety symptoms.

Increased perplexity in life could also result from a blocked third eye chakra. Admittedly, most of us navigate life bewildered by the many options available. The world is becoming more chaotic and information-rich, so it's reasonable to feel overwhelmed and bewildered. That being stated, you may have a blocked third eye chakra if you notice you feel more confused than usual. Paying attention to what you previously believed you had clarity will help you grasp this. Were there any decisions that you found particularly easy to make? Have those options recently grown more intimidating in any way? If the answer is yes, there's a chance that your third eye chakra isn't aligned properly.

Dreams and sleep are other areas that the third eye chakra impacts. We've seen how closely this chakra is related to the pineal gland, which regulates our sleep-wake cycles. We may experience irregular sleep patterns when this chakra becomes obstructed. In severe circumstances, we can even have to deal with sleeplessness. Worries might also be an indication of a blocked chakra. You may need to align your third eye chakra if you've noticed a significant shift in the quality or timing of your sleep.

The third eye chakra can also give us the impression that we are in charge of our dreams when aligned (more on this coming). When our dreams are obstructed, they might take over our lives and interfere with our everyday responsibilities. You may be experiencing difficulties balancing your third eye chakra if you observe an increased propensity to daydream.

It's acceptable to occasionally feel disconnected from both your mental and exterior worlds, and feeling out of rhythm with oneself is quite normal. However, you may need to examine yourself if you're having trouble connecting with your mission or finding it over time. Your vision must make sense to you; it need not be expansive or "important." While overcoming life's obstacles daily is vital, having something bigger to aim for is just as crucial. Without it, we may feel like we're just existing.

This symptom and the previous one are connected. A blocked third eye chakra may cause your feelings of being stuck in life and lacking motivation. A third eye chakra that is aligned can provide us with the confidence we need to focus on our abilities and objectives, as well as help us see our way. You may need to concentrate on clearing your third eye chakra if you get stuck in a pattern you can't seem to break out from.

Additionally, the seat of creativity and imagination is the third eye chakra. You may feel very limited in your creativity when this chakra is obstructed. Put differently, you may find it difficult to generate new ideas or to work on any of them. You may even struggle with diverse and critical thinking.

You can tell if you have trouble using your imagination by considering how you handle uncertainty and scarcity. Creative individuals, for instance, are typically adept at making the most of little time or resources. True creative people may even welcome constraints to expand their creative potential. This is demonstrated by the well-known Oulipo tradition, in which writers and mathematicians of French descent exploited constraints to produce thought-provoking works. One well-known example is Georges Perec's work A Void, written entirely sans the letter "e."

That's a challenging task in our regular written correspondence, let alone when writing a novel, as you may understand. Nonetheless, these writers thought that limiting their work would make them more inventive and better writers. Compare this mindset to someone always whining about not having the resources or environment needed to produce. Should you be in this group, you may need to focus on aligning your third eye chakra.

This chakra instills optimism and hope since it is associated with the world of possibilities. I'm not referring to poisonous or forced positivism here, where you must deceive yourself into thinking things will work out. We know everything will work out since we're on the correct track when we see ourselves and our lives. Put differently, we can perceive our challenges and disappointments more impartially and favorably. But when this chakra is closed, the world can seem like it's about to swallow us whole. If you often ask yourself, "What's the point?" or if you feel incredibly negative most of the time, your third eye chakra may be blocked."

This chakra is associated with serenity and sleep. Hence, an imbalanced chakra can lead to a variety of emotional problems. Anxiety and stress levels might also rise as a result of disrupted sleep cycles. You may occasionally need to cope with paranoia and sadness as well. You may also have a pessimistic outlook on life. In other situations, you can begin to assume the worst. So they can help you understand your underlying thought patterns.

Analyze your beliefs to see how your third eye chakra is feeling. Have they recently developed an excessive sense of logic or reason? Do you attempt to "make sense" of everything that occurs to you or those in your immediate vicinity? Are you willing to offer logical justifications for everything that looks unusual or hard to explain? If so, there's a chance that your third eye chakra is obstructed. The tendency to become extremely emotional in various situations is on the other end of the scale. We may not see things clearly, which is a sign that the chakra is blocked, whether we're buried in our emotions or removed from them.

While many of us may not naturally hold spiritual views, we might nonetheless be receptive to them. If nothing else, we ought to be able to handle issues that are difficult to answer without getting intimidated by them. Spiritual inquiries are meant to elicit discomfort from humans by definition. That's perfectly OK. The issue appears when we avoid having spiritual conversations at all. If we flee from anything that isn't entirely tangible, we may need to focus on opening our third eye chakra.

What kind of relationships do you have with those around you? Do you prefer to keep things as surface-level as possible while conversing with the people in your life, or are you comfortable having meaningful and in-depth conversations? Of course, having these kinds of discussions with strangers or people you don't feel particularly connected to is neither feasible nor wise. That being said, you may have a blocked third eye chakra if you find it difficult to do this with anyone, including individuals who are open to such concepts. Generally speaking, your third eye chakra may be blocked if you find it difficult to connect with others or trust them.

We may experience higher levels of irritation or rage than usual when our third eye chakra is blocked or when we are first beginning the process of chakra awakening. It may surprise you if, in the past, you have worked hard on yourself and even extended forgiveness to those who have harmed you. Suddenly, you may find yourself reliving old memories, particularly the traumatic ones, and coping with the negative feelings that accompany them. Similarly, you may notice less tolerance for other people's shortcomings. You might even act haughty, entitled, or better than others in severe circumstances. We experience a dissolution of our ego and a sense of community when our third eye chakra is aligned. Our ego takes the front stage in our lives when it's blocked. You might even become stubborn and stiff when it comes to your convictions.

Because the third eye chakra is associated with intuition, having a blocked chakra can negatively impact our intuitive abilities. You may occasionally find it difficult to believe your instincts. You may struggle to understand what your inner voice is saying to you and feel disoriented and lost. You may have to ignore your instincts even if they tell you anything. In other situations, you may need to deal with feelings of approaching disaster. Stated differently, your intuition may alert you to a problem even if you cannot identify it.

(Take a two-second break.)

Return your focus to the here and now. Now, you will clear the Muladhara chakra using a visualization approach. Red symbolizes the root chakra, also known as the Muladhara chakra. Imagine the Muladhara chakra now as a crimson dot or Bindu. Examine the red

Bindu steadily expanding in your mind's eye. Allow the color red to envelop your entire lower abdomen. The color red represents energy that is dormant and ready to be released.

(Hold off for ten seconds.)

Sensate the heat that the red hue spreads across your pelvis. This heat is energy, plain and simple. This energy is the original energy that all living things possess. Animals are not exempt from it. In humans, the mind transforms this instinctive force into joy and the realization of the truth.

Allow your pelvic region's heat to contract and return to a dot. Sensate the transformation of the intense heat into the smallest form possible: an atom. The red heat is getting progressively less. As you can see, the Muladhara chakra is fusing with the crimson fire.

(Hold off for ten seconds.)

The dot is getting smaller and more subtle. It's no longer within your mental image. The heat is only detectable to you. Hold this position for five seconds. The exercise should then be done five times.

(Take a 30-second break.)

You might not be able to feel the heat in your lower abdomen at first. To effortlessly bring on the sensations of heat and cold with just your willpower takes a lot of practice. Your body is a magnificent machine.

You can use your mind to do superhuman feats. You need to have total faith in the procedure and the fortitude to see it through to the end without having any concerns.

Reconnect your consciousness with your physical body now. Return your focus to your breathing. It is necessary to breathe in and out normally. Relax your entire body. Feel a powerful, energizing rush through your body.

(Hold off for ten seconds.)

You are feeling a new energy in the clearing and healing of the Muladhara chakra. You experience vitality and activity. Your mission in life has changed due to the restoration of the Muladharachakra. Now, your idle ideas and future goals are beginning to take shape.

You could apply this limitless power source directly to building a prosperous existence. You can also use this energy to open more chakras, which will help you achieve more ambitious life goals. Stay in this blissful condition for a while. Your pelvic region's warmth and heat must go away on its own. Allow the quitting process to unfold naturally over time.

(Hold off for a minute.)

Return your focus to your body when the timing is right for you. Step with your feet slowly. Make a finger movement. You can relax in your seating position. It is no longer necessary to clear and cure the Muladhara chakra.

Prayer and Sacred Sexuality

Combining Joy and Love in a Sacred Partnership

Sacred sexuality invites us to feel divine connection via the physical act of love. It is a profound spiritual practice that unites the domains of pleasure and devotion. Through deliberate sexual acts as a kind of prayer, we can transcend our own identities and become one with the divine. Sacred sexuality can be accepted as a spiritual practice in the following ways:

Purposeful Association:

Set aside time to cultivate a sacred and safe environment for your partner's sexual exploration. Focus on conscious and loving connection. Aim to honor and establish a connection with the divine within each other by approaching the event with reverence.

Being Aware:

When making love, practice mindful presence and permit yourself to completely lose yourself in the surface of feelings and energies. Give up all objectives and expectations and give yourself to the divine flow of connection and joy.

Heart-Based Cooperation:

Take heart-centered exercises to strengthen your emotional and energetic bond with your spouse, such as holding hands, synchronized breathing, or eye gazing. Develop a sense of profound love, trust, and openness as your energies unite in a holy union.

Gratitude and Prayer:

Incorporate spiritual exercises and prayer into your sex life. Thank the almighty for the blessings of enjoyment and companionship. Take part in fervent prayers, positive affirmations, or hallowed chants to enhance the spiritual aspects of the encounter.

You can reach the profound spiritual layers of your existence and transcend the physical realm by uniting pleasure and dedication in a sacred union. You create a space for the expression and experience of divine love, pleasure, and spiritual connection through holy sexuality.

Ecstatic Experiences as a Path to a Higher Self: Examining the Mystic Aspects of Sensuality

We can enter ecstasies through sensuality and establish direct communication with the divine. We pass beyond the ego's bounds and into a mystical world of transcendence and unification during these elevated moments of sensual delight. The following are some approaches to investigating the esoteric aspects of sensuality:

Kundalini Awakening and Tantra

Explore the connection of sexual energy and spiritual awakening via the techniques of Kundalini Yoga and Tantra. You can feel the union of the divine masculine and feminine inside yourself and awaken the Kundalini energy through breathwork, visualization, and holy ceremonies.

Engaging in Meditation and Sensory Focusing

Practice sensory-focused meditations in which you focus on the energy and feelings that arise in your body. You can create space for great spiritual experiences by practicing deep presence and attunement to your senses.

ecstatic movement and dance

Examine the healing potential of ecstatic movement and dance. Give yourself over to the beat of the music and let your body speak for itself naturally. You can achieve trance-like states through unrestrained movement when you become one with the holy energy.

Customs of Devotion and Abandonment:

Make rituals unique to you and represent your surrender to the almighty. During sensuous rituals, this can involve using religious objects, lighting candles, or burning incense. Practice surrender; give yourself over to the divine presence both inside and around you.

Consciously participating in these activities allows the mystical aspects of sensuality to surface. You dissolve the limitations of the self and become one with the divine essence that penetrates everything through ecstasy experiences. Spiritual direction, and realize all things' tremendous connection and interconnectedness during these transcendent moments.

You set off on a path of spiritual enlightenment and growing connection with the divine when you accept sensuality as a practice. By incorporating sensuality into your current spiritual practices, exploring the mystical aspects of sensuality, and fusing pleasure and devotion in holy sexuality, you can achieve tremendous spiritual growth, expansion, and enlightenment.

Sensuality as a spiritual discipline offers a very individualized and profoundly transformational path to the divine. Through this holy voyage, you awaken the latent parts of yourself, reveal the joyous essence of life, and develop a close relationship with the divine presence inside and around you. Accept sensuality as a doorway to spiritual enlightenment, and let the flames of divine connection guide you towards self-awareness, adoration, and oneness with the divine.

ACADEMY OF LIFE

"The Battle of Life cannot be won by fighting but by understanding."

The only people who truly understand how difficult life is are those who are now living it. There are only two options available to those who are experiencing pain, stress, or illnesses: either embrace challenges as a chance to gain insight into life and discover its mysteries, or get lost in the maze of their problems, believing themselves to be unlucky, and taking their own life.

In 1979, I was born into a modest household consisting of my mother Lakshmi and father Prakash in the small village of Choutpally, located in the former Andhra Pradesh state in India. I had to deal with a lot of issues in my life ever since I was little. I had stomach pains for twenty years. This made it impossible for me to enjoy life in any way—I could not focus on my schoolwork, eat healthily, sleep soundly, or advance.

I spent a long time taking medications. I continued to visit hospitals, seeking advice from numerous knowledgeable medical professionals and well-wishers. However, I was unable to locate a solution anywhere. I could not get better. I made all the exterior treatment-related efforts that needed to be made wherever I had to go. There was no hope, and nothing worked. In addition to my physical challenges, my family was also dealing with a lot of social and financial difficulties, which made me very depressed since I was a little child and made me lose interest in life. Anger began to bubble up in my head. I couldn't stop asking myself why my family and I were experiencing this every second. What went wrong with me? I was thinking about these questions day and night.

When there was no external remedy, I turned my attention inward. I tried to comprehend who I was by drawing on my knowledge of numerous old spiritual works of literature.

I spent a long time trying to comprehend my subconscious's makeup, habits, and depth. I got to work on it based on what I knew. My life and personality started to gradually change after that.

My spouse and I founded the Shivganeshyoga Foundation Trust to provide individuals with the same expertise. For the past 12 years, we have worked to raise awareness and educate the public through various public programs. I have no idea how many others throughout the world deal with issues similar to mine, endure illnesses, and find themselves in precarious circumstances. On this, lakhs of rupees are being spent. Nevertheless, they are unable to enjoy life or get healthy. This book was produced with the intention that everyone will be able to enjoy a happy and healthy life. May they all acquire this knowledge.

I have personally encountered every enigmatic concept and method described in this book. These are the universe's eternal laws and our sages' discoveries. With this enigmatic supernatural knowledge repository, you can find an eternal answer to any problem, regardless of the type of ailment.

THE GREATEST GUARANTEE

"If you're looking to unlock the mysteries of the universe, consider energy, frequency, and vibration."

- Nikola Tesla

The earth is full of all kinds of energies. Each has vibrational frequency and effects, including gravitational, electrical, thermal, and chemical energy. It is a human person who has found all of these different kinds of energies. That person is also a living being. There is a frequency and vibration to this energy or existence, and this quality is known as self-consciousness.

To decipher the mysteries of the cosmos, we must examine human energy levels, which are divided into just two types. There are two: the "sub-conscious" and the "conscious."

"conscious" refers to self-driven energy and awareness independent of other influences. The term "subconscious" or "unconscious" refers to energy that cannot move independently and is instead dependent on other forces.

Put another way, we can think of the universe as a conscious form known as Brahma Mahatattva, or cosmic energy. In the tangible world, the unconscious is considered as matter.

We don't need to look outside the physical realm to find the answers to the universe's hidden secrets. We only need to turn inward for inspiration.

Just consider this. Humans walk, eat, drink, and so on. Who are we actually, and what are we living? What occurs after a death? Why don't people store what is referred to as a dead body in their homes? Why does the other person take the person he has loved and been with for a long time out of the house while that person is lying in the form of a body?

Because the person is unconscious and their body is lying in front of them. The body no longer contains the conscious being that formerly controlled it; it has vanished. It was the soul within that mattered.

The energy that propels and regulates the body is known in science as aware energy. This implies that the energy known as the soul keeps the body, composed of five elements, alive.

Has anyone seen the soul, that aware being?

While the body can be seen, consciousness cannot. It cannot be seen because it is invisible. Consequently, the soul is an energy and the greatest mystery that must be solved first. The universe's mysteries are concealed within this.

Thus, one thing is evident to us in this situation: invisible energy, which is what is doing everything, is invisible. However, where does it originate from is the question. How far does it travel? Nobody is aware of this. However, individuals who were aware of this secret and comprehended it had a lasting impact on the entire planet.

Because they were aware of their energy level, identity, and life's Purpose.

Chakra II/Sacral (Svadhishthana)

This chakra, Svadhishthana (Sanskrit for "dwelling place of the Self"), is situated in the navel, precisely between the pelvic bones. The sacral chakra helps you create the life you want. It is typically symbolized by orange, which stands for rising consciousness, purity, and activity. Joy, passion, faith, self-assurance, and equilibrium are brought about by its vitality. The sacral chakra, the seat of passion, facilitates the development of close relationships and helps awaken your creativity and emotional well-being.

This chakra, associated with water, stands for flexibility and flow. Its energy supports letting go, embracing transformation, and accepting change. Thus, it is linked to various psychological and mental processes, including emotions (such as pleasure), creativity, and the urge to interact with others. The ovaries, testicles, bladder, kidneys, and sexual/reproductive organs are all associated with this chakra.

A misaligned sacral chakra can manifest as low self-esteem, co-dependency, separation from oneself, depression, asthma, allergies, food disorders, addiction to substances and behavioral habits (such as drug, gambling, or alcohol use), and even physical issues. An unbalanced sacral chakra manifests as compulsive behavior and a fear of losing relationship control. The imbalance also impacts the relationship with other facets of life, including job and career.

Celebrate and value your accomplishments, small and large, as well as those of others, to align this chakra. Consume orange foods (carrots, oranges, etc.), wear orange clothing, and surround yourself with romantic media (music, movies, and literature). Approach the water by swimming or strolling by a lake, river, or sea. Treat yourself to lengthy, opulent baths with fragrant candles, tanning, or anything else that makes you happy. Additionally, essential oils like ylang-ylang can be used to balance and treat this chakra.

Manipura's Third/Solar Plexus Chakra

On the stomach, above the navel, is the solar plexus chakra. The Sanskrit term for Manipura is "a lustrous gem," and yellow is typically associated with this chakra. The fire element of this chakra is associated with positive vibration, self-worth, confidence, and personal power. Thus, this is where your strength and confidence come through. This energy center produces heat from the body, which helps digestion when you light the fire within it. The solar plexus chakra focuses on the strength and independence of metabolism while fortifying the diaphragm and digestive system.

Yellow is a color that symbolizes youth, rebirth, birth, energy, intelligence, and your connection to fire and the sun. Those drawn to yellow are typically interested in intellectual endeavors, as this color is associated with intellect and wisdom. Love and happiness rise to the heart chakra. The fire element encourages a bright consciousness, pushing you toward prosperity and well-being.

The pancreas, gallbladder, and brain are connected to the digestive system, liver, and chakra. Digestion issues, poor memory, anxiety, impulsive behavior (aggression, wrath, etc.), and mental blockage or imbalance can all appear when things are out of alignment.

Yoga, yellow attire, yellow foods (bananas, yellow bell peppers, etc.), sunshine, and yellow materials and items around you are some of the most efficient ways to rebalance this chakra. Additionally, you can awaken the solar plexus chakra by affirming oneself through meditation and positive language. When this energy center is balanced, you feel self-inspired, confident, and excited to fulfill your life's Purpose.

Anahata, the Fourth/Heart Chakra

The Heart Heart symbolizes love, compassion, trust, and passion and represents the equilibrium between the upper and lower chakras. Emotions and touch are physically linked to the heart. You feel pleasant, upbeat, friendly, and self-inspired when your HeartHeart is open. It's simple to keep up loving, satisfying partnerships. The heart chakra is related to forgiveness, compassion, self-acceptance, and love—the capacity to love without conditions.

The fourth chakra is thought to be the most important of the seven energy centers. Here is where you open your HeartHeart to give and receive freely. The word Anahata (Sanskrit for "unbeaten" or "unstuck") refers to the HeartHeart, which stands for the unconditional love that brings to a greater comprehension of oneself and other people. Having an open heart makes it easier to consider many kinds and levels of relationship experiences.

The heart chakra, which stands for freedom and expansion, is associated with green and air elements. This chakra cultivates a consciousness that leads to boundless compassion. Green symbolizes achievement, personal development, and happy, fulfilling relationships. It also stands for warmth, freshness, nature, and tenderness. Green is linked to strength, stability, tranquility, balance, peace, and compassion. It is also a soothing color for the human eye.

Emotional symptoms, including jealousy, irritability, fear, anxiety, and lack of trust, can occur when this chakra is out of balance. You experience love, compassion, optimism, kindness, and inspiration when you are in balance. The heart, lungs, liver, and immune system are the linked organs; high blood pressure and love-related emotional challenges may arise from an imbalance in this chakra.

The heart chakra can be balanced by going back to yourself, forgiving yourself, relaxing through artistic endeavors (like painting mandalas), regular breathing exercises like AnulomVilom (see chapter 4, page 124), spending time in nature, surrounding yourself with greenery, consuming green foods (broccoli, avocado, and leafy greens, for example), and employing appropriate natural stones and crystals. Strong relationships are facilitated by self-knowledge, aided by a balanced heart chakra.

The System of Chakras:

The seven primary chakras that make up the chakra system are arranged from the base of the spine to the top of the head along the body's center channel. Certain attributes, elements, colors, and functions are connected to each chakra. Knowing the qualities of each chakra is essential to understanding how they affect our overall health.

Muladhara, the root chakra:

Situated at the base of the spine, the root chakra is linked to our sense of steadiness, safety, and earthly connection. It is associated with the earth element and represented by the color red. The root chakra offers a strong base for our mental and physical health.

Svadhishthana, the sacral chakra:

The lower abdomen's sacral chakra is associated with creativity, sexuality, and emotional expression. It controls our capacity for enjoyment, adaptability to change, and building wholesome connections. This chakra is linked to the element of water, and orange is the color that represents it.

Belly is associated with our willpower, self-worth, and inner strength. It affects our capacity to decide what to do, materialize our desires, and act. This chakra is linked to the element of fire, and yellow is the color that represents it.

Anahata, the heart chakra:

The lower and upper chakras are connected by the heart chakra, which is located in the middle of the chest. It controls our ability to show and accept forgiveness, compassion, and love. The heart chakra impacts our connections to the divine, our emotional health, and our relationships. This chakra is linked to the element of air, and green is the color that represents it.

The Vishuddha Chakra (throat):

Self-expression, communication, and genuineness. It controls our ability to confidently communicate our feelings, thoughts, and truths. This chakra is linked to the element of sound, and blue is the color that represents it.

Ajna, the Third Eye Chakra:

It is associated with inner wisdom, awareness, and intuition. It controls our capacity to reach greater insight, spiritual knowledge, and consciousness. This chakra is linked to the element of light, and indigo is the color that represents it.

Sahasrara, the crown chakra, is

The top of the head is home to the crown chakra, which stands for our link to enlightenment, global intelligence, and divine consciousness. It unites us with the infinite and the divine and transcends individuality. This chakra is linked to the element of mind; it can be represented by the colors violet or white.

Energy Flow and Chakras:

Chakras are entry points via which energy from our subtle body can pass. Prana flows freely via balanced and open chakras, promoting health, vitality, and spiritual development. On the other hand, energy flow can be disturbed by blockages or imbalances in the chakras, which can result in difficulties with the body, mind, and soul.

Disproportions in Chakras:

Several things, including stress, trauma, negative emotions, poor lifestyle choices, and energetic disturbances, can lead to chakra imbalances. An overactive, underactive, or obstructed chakra can show itself as emotional instability, physical problems, or isolation from the outside world.

Chakra Harmony and Equilibrium:

Chakra healing aims to bring the chakras back into harmony and balance, allowing energy to flow freely and enhancing general well-being. Using various healing techniques and modalities, such as energy healing, yoga, affirmations, crystals, meditation, and aromatherapy.

Our subtle bodies contain strong energy centers called chakras that impact our mental, emotional, and spiritual states. Knowing the chakra system gives us a better understanding of our interconnectedness and allows us to develop harmony, balance, and energy. In the upcoming chapters, we will go into great detail on each chakra, along with helpful hints and activities to help you on your path to self-discovery and chakra healing. Recall that you can experience deep transformation and embark on a journey of personal development and spiritual awareness by accepting the teachings of the chakras.

"To make other people happy, show sympathy for them. To get happiness, cultivate compassion.

— DALAI LAMA

You can become compassionate and loving by developing your Heart chakra after trying to balance your Solar Plexus chakra and grow personally. You can nurture stronger feelings of empathy and unconditional love by repairing your HeartHeart. A balanced heart pushes you beyond your egoistic worries to an awareness of others and the needs of everyone. This opens the door to deeper qualities of service to the community around you.

We can easily give and receive love, feel surrounded by love, and genuinely connect and accept others and ourselves when our Heart Centre is open and balanced. Our interactions in general, especially our love ties with partners, are impacted by the health of this chakra. Compassion, empathy, trust, and balanced love—all attributes of a balanced Heart chakra—are the cornerstones of a robust, wholesome relationship or partnership.

A striking and potent sculpture depicting a struggle in a relationship between two loved ones was on display during the 2015 Burning Man Festival. Alexander Milov's artwork, "Love," featured two wire-frame adults sitting with their backs to one another in anguish following a disagreement. Two kids, symbolizing the "inner child" of each relationship, were positioned inside the wire-frame sculpture, reaching out to touch each other despite the exterior bodies' disdain and wrath. This "demonstrates the outer and inner expression of human nature," according to Milov.

Even though growing older brings many wonderful blessings, our adult propensity to let pride, criticism, and bitterness win in a fight is not good for our souls. Our actual nature is our inner child's kind, free-spirited, and forgiving spirit. When did you last lose your temper with a loved one because you could not choose empathy, compassion, or love? How did you say that? In what way did you say it? What emotions did you experience?

Many of us find it simple to snap and allow our rage to get the better of us when it comes to someone we care about. After the fact, we frequently need to cut off contact with the other person because we are furious and annoyed and believe we have been misinterpreted. But what we want is to connect, maybe very, really deep down. It can be quite challenging to acknowledge what your inner self thinks and desires and see past feelings of rage, irritation, and resentment. The Heart and Throat chakras are related when we experience these conflicts (more on the Throat chakra in the following guide). Consider these chakras to delve further and investigate various facets of your life and inner world.

The "lone wolf" archetype becomes an intriguing idea when we consider the Heart and Solar Plexus chakras.

Individuals who exhibit traits associated with this archetype are commonly called "hyper-individualistic" or "ultra-independent" healers. They are proud of their detachment and see their extreme independence as vital to who they are. The lone wolf archetype is useful for the ego because it indicates an overactive Solar Plexus chakra, which keeps us from opening up and mending our Heart center.

As the person "sets strong boundaries" and "protects their energy," this ultra-independent path may seem to be "healing," but in reality, it is a sealing of the entryways that lead to the HeartHeart. We run a significant risk when we allow ourselves to be vulnerable and open to connection with others. We give up some of the power that keeps us feeling safe when we go into a relationship, and we frequently have to confront the most vulnerable and afraid aspects of ourselves, which are easier to ignore when we are by ourselves. But never forget that opening your Heart is WORTH IT. Avoid becoming mired in the third chakra; while vulnerability, love, and compassion are all important aspects of our power, so is independence.

To experience real growth and healing, one must be vulnerable. Vulnerability can be understood as our ability to be injured because the word vulnerability is derived from the Latin word vulnerability, which means "to wound." Humans are inherently vulnerable from the moment of conception until the moment of death. But as author and speaker Dr. Gabor Maté noted on Jay Shetty's podcast On Purpose, when we are harmed as children, and the vulnerability becomes unbearable, we attempt to suppress our vulnerability. We might accomplish this by constantly "being right" because we think that if we are right, we are strong and will be protected from the suffering that comes with vulnerability. But we cease evolving when we act in this way.

Everything in nature only grows when it is fragile, as Dr.Maté notes. Trees develop only when soft, green, and fragile; a crustacean animal, such as a crab inside a hard shell, can only grow when it molds and becomes extremely susceptible. We must let go of the defenses we developed as kids to shield ourselves from hurt, like being correct to be vulnerable. For this reason, the idea of "growing pains" exists; development cannot occur without vulnerability.

The first four to seven years of childhood are crucial for the development and "programming" of the Heart chakra, as this is the time when we learn the necessary behaviors and self-image to win others' love and acceptance. As children, we might witness friends, family members, and/or siblings being treated differently due to their deeds. Kids will acquire the ability to reject and "disown" aspects of themselves that they do not believe to be "acceptable" or worthy of affection, depending on their experiences during this developmental stage.

Parents and guardians could not even be aware of it, yet they might not love or accept one child more than another, depending on specific behaviors. These "conditions" for love and acceptance develop children's self-perceptions and opinions of others. They also foster subconscious anxieties of not being loved or accepted if certain requirements are not "met," which can lead to blockages in the heart chakra that can last into adulthood.

We must process our grief and sadness to heal and bring the Heart Centre back into equilibrium. A common metaphor for the "shadow side" of the heart chakra is grief, which prevents energy from flowing through this region. When someone or something is taken away from us, even a part of who we are or the person we thought we wanted to be, we experience grief. When we have to accept that something is no longer an option in our lives, we also experience grief from the loss of possibilities. It's a highly complicated feeling that may sometimes be overwhelming, bringing more challenging and sometimes unanticipated feelings, including deep sadness, rage, regret, guilt, and disbelief.

It is well known that the Heart chakra governs our capacity for love. This chakra is the doorway to all forms of love, including Divine love. Still, to access it, we must be willing to consider the potential of sadness and grief and have the fortitude to overcome these difficulties.

It can be very challenging for those who are grieving to keep their HeartHeart open, undefended, and unimpeded when their intellect is telling them to shut it off from the agony. By practicing heart-opening yoga poses, reflecting and meditating, repeating affirmations, and other heart-opening techniques, you can work on opening and healing your Heart chakra and perhaps find a deeper love that will reveal a "sweetness" in this loss. A greater comprehension of how your recovery journey has led you here through your grief and loss. As you can see, one of its goals is to teach you to accept and be receptive to life as it comes, with all of its hardships and sorrows. It will also reveal to you previously hidden aspects of your inner self. One of John Green's best quotes is, "Grief does not change you." It makes you clear." Furthermore, it directs you. You will become someone you could never have been without this loss, led by your sadness.

The Power of Holy Sounds: The mantras are considered extremely potent and holy and are typically composed of carefully chosen syllables or phrases in ancient languages such as Sanskrit. Mantras are sound vibrations that carry inherent energies that can change an individual's mental and emotional condition and the environment in which they are used. Mantras are chanted continuously to help clear the mind, increase energy, and align the practitioner with higher spiritual vibrations.

Aspects of Meditation and Devotion: There are two main methods to do mantra yoga: as a means of introspection or as a way to demonstrate devotion. In contemplative meditation, the practitioner focuses on the mind and transcends conventional notions by repeating the mantra with focused concentration. Mantras are sung with great reverence and love for the divine as a holy activity, creating a sense of surrender and a connection to the sacred.

Universal and Inclusive Practice: Mantra yoga's adaptability is one of its great qualities. Although mantras have their roots in Buddhism, Hinduism, and other ancient traditions, people of different spiritual backgrounds and faiths can use them. Mantras have a vibrational power that cuts beyond cultural boundaries, making them useful for anybody pursuing self-realization and spiritual advancement.

Mantra Progression And The Guru-Disciple Bond

Certain lineages believe that a mantra's effectiveness depends on having it recited by a qualified spiritual instructor or "Guru." The spiritual essence of the Guru is infused into the mantra through this initiation process, which creates a sacred bond between the pupil and the teacher. It is crucial to follow the guidance of the Guru to properly recite the mantra and maximize its potency.

Goals & Objectives of Mantra Yoga: Overcoming ego limitations and realizing the interconnectedness of all things is the ultimate goal of mantra yoga. With regular practice, practitioners can achieve a variety of spiritual goals, such as:

1. Self-realization: Realising the divine inside and discovering one's true nature.

2. Spiritual Growth: Making headway towards enlightenment and spiritual advancement.

3. Emotional Stability: Realising inner peace, harmony, and tranquility.

4. Divine Connection: Connecting with a higher power or a global consciousness.

5. Healing and Purification: Eliminating negative energy and undesirable habits from the body and psyche.

6. Transformation: Letting go of constrictive beliefs and thought patterns.

Integration with Daily Life: Mantra yoga is a style of meditation that may be used in everyday situations, going beyond structured sessions. Practitioners can maintain awareness, gratitude, and a sense of presence by repeating mantras while performing routine tasks. Mantras can also show compassion and love for others or offer positive energy in the face of adversity.

To put it briefly, Mantra Yoga is a deep spiritual practice that involves repeating sacred sounds or words to stimulate spiritual growth, awaken higher states of awareness, and strengthen spiritual ties. It is a potent and all-encompassing practice that can support spiritual growth in individuals with various backgrounds and worldviews.

1.2 Mantra Yoga's Origins and History

With roots dating back thousands of years, Mantra Yoga deeply connects to the diverse spiritual and philosophical traditions throughout the Indian subcontinent. It is necessary to comprehend the development of mantras, their sacred significance, and how they were incorporated into other spiritual practices to comprehend the origins and history of Mantra Yoga.

Ancient Initiations: Mantra yoga has its roots in prehistoric rituals and ceremonies involving singing, chanting, and rhythmic sound production by early human communities. These archaic ceremonies demonstrated reverence for the natural world, the cosmos, and the unseen forces affecting human existence. The fact that sound-making is repetitive perhaps contributed to realizing its transformational power over emotions and consciousness.

Vedic Era (1500 BCE–500 BCE): The Vedic era began around 1500 BCE when Mantra Yoga first gained traction. During this Period, several hymns, prayers, and chants were included in the Vedas, a collection of religious texts. During religious ceremonies, these mantras were chanted to call upon certain deities, ask for blessings, and obtain protection. Mantras, which harnessed the power of sound, were an essential component of Vedic rites and were thought to be an effective means of establishing a close spiritual connection.

Upanishadic Period (800–200 BCE): During this time, the focus of spiritual inquiry shifted from ceremonial rites to more in-depth philosophical inquiries into the nature of reality, the self, and the cosmos. The philosophical works known as the Upanishads, which came after the Vedas, explored a profound comprehension of "Brahman," or ultimate truth, and "Atman," or the true self. The significance of sound as a transformative tool for grasping these concepts was emphasized in texts such as the Mandukya Upanishad, which presented the sound "AUM" as the fundamental sound that represents Brahman.

Tantra development (c. 300–1200 CE):

An important turning point in the development of Mantra Yoga was the emergence of Tantric traditions. Tantras were mystical texts that explored the mystical aspects of spirituality and emphasized the role of sounds, symbols, and rituals in a person's spiritual awakening. Tantric practitioners acknowledged the potential of mantras to achieve spiritual liberation and activate subtle energies (Kundalini).

These traditions resulted in a deeper comprehension of mantra yoga as a liberating and transformative spiritual practice.

Ajna, the Third Eye Chakra

One of the seven primary chakras in the human body, the Third Eye Chakra (called Ajna in Sanskrit), is in the middle of the forehead. It is connected to the elements of light and the color indigo. Scientifically speaking, the pineal gland—a tiny endocrine gland located in the brain's center that secretes melatonin—is connected to the Third Eye Chakra. In addition to controlling sleep-wake cycles, this hormone affects the immune system and circadian rhythms.

The Third Eye Chakra is attributed to our capacity to access our intuition, insight, and psychic powers. It is linked to traits like inventiveness, wisdom, and intuition. As the seat of consciousness, this chakra establishes a connection with our higher selves. Third Eye Chakra imbalances can lead to a lack of clarity or intuition, trouble making decisions, and separation from one's spiritual or intuitive nature. A third eye chakra imbalance can manifest physically as headaches, vision issues, and sleep disturbances.

Various methods, including energy healing, visualization, and meditation, can balance the Third Eye Chakra. Accessing higher states of consciousness and calming the mind are two benefits of meditation. Visualization exercises can awaken and stimulate the Third Eye Chakra, increasing insight and clarity. Acupuncture and Reiki are energy-healing techniques that help balance the chakras and enhance well-being.

A lotus flower with two petals, either blue or indigo, commonly represents the Third Eye Chakra. These two petals symbolize the dual and non-dual elements of consciousness.

Sahasrara, or the crown chakra

The highest and most divine chakra in the human body is the Crown Chakra, sometimes called Sahasrara. Located near the top of the head, it is linked to the element of mind and the color violet. Consciousness is attributed to it.

Physically, the pineal gland, which controls our mood, aging process, and sleep-wake cycle, is connected to the Crown Chakra.

The Crown Chakra symbolizes our innate spirituality and capacity to acquire transcendental knowledge and insight. It gives us a profound sense of unity with the cosmos and our position and is said to be the seat of our highest consciousness and enlightenment.

Increased spiritual awareness, a closer bond with our inner guidance and intuition, and a stronger feeling of purpose and fulfillment can all be brought about by a balanced Crown

Chakra. On the other hand, mental and physical symptoms like despair, sleeplessness, and a loss of connection to our higher self can result from an imbalanced Crown Chakra.

To balance and activate the Crown Chakra, several practices, including yoga, meditation, and prayer, can help us develop a stronger connection to our higher consciousness and relieve physical strain. A thousand-petaled lotus flower is a common representation of the Crown Chakra, signifying consciousness's boundless and infinite nature.

Advantages

It reduces tension, headaches, and physical, mental, and emotional discomfort. The blood is purified by it. It lessens bruises and edoema. It improves the endocrine system and metabolism. It treats various gastrointestinal issues, cellular illnesses, skin conditions, and ailments affecting the lungs and respiratory systems. It eases melancholy and loss.

Positioning

You can wear this as jewelry, particularly around your heart or throat. Geodes and clusters can be arranged throughout your house. To help with insomnia, you might put it under your pillow. Healing usually involves the usage of single points. If left in direct sunlight, it will fade.

Defense

It is a very shielding stone. It has potent healing and purifying properties. It dispels unfavorable energy from the surroundings. It guards against nightmares that come again. It fosters selflessness and a love of the holy.

[Source]

East Africa, Uruguay, India, Brazil, Sri Lanka, Mexico, Canada, Britain, and the United States.

As its name implies, moonstone has a close relationship with the moon. It is a symbol of fresh starts. It improves one's psychic powers. It calms and stabilizes emotions and has a very relaxing impact. It thereby encourages profound emotional recovery. It lessens shock.

Hyperactive children can benefit from it.

Advantages

It helps the body retain fluids and gets rid of contaminants. It helps the reproductive and digestive systems. It comforts PMS, conception, pregnancy, childbirth, and nursing. It relieves degenerative liver, pancreas, hair, eyes, and skin disorders. Additionally, sleeplessness can be treated with it.

Positioning

You can wear it as a ring or pendant, or you can wear it wherever appropriate on the body. You can place it on the forehead for spiritual experiences, the solar plexus chakra, or the heart for emotions. Women might need to avoid wearing it during a full moon.

Defense

It eases overreaction to situations by calming the emotions. It is brimming with passive, receptive feminine energy. It, therefore, harmonizes the energy of men and women. It will help guys connect with their inner femininity. For extremely aggressive ladies and hypermasculine men, it is the ideal stone.

www.ingramcontent.com/pod-product-compliance
Lightning Source LLC
Chambersburg PA
CBHW052135110526
44591CB00012B/1729